SHARKS
and Other Wild Water Animals
Four Underwater Stories

Chomp! A Book About Sharks
Splash! A Book About Whales and Dolphins
Dive! A Book of Deep-Sea Creatures
Snap! A Book About Alligators and Crocodiles

SCHOLASTIC INC.
Cartwheel ·B·O·O·K·S· ®
New York Toronto London Auckland Sydney
Mexico City New Delhi Hong Kong Buenos Aires

Chomp! A Book About Sharks (0-590-52298-1)
Text copyright © 1999 by Melvin Berger.

Splash! A Book About Whales and Dolphins (0-439-20166-7)
Text copyright © 2001 by Melvin & Gilda Berger.

Dive! A Book of Deep-Sea Creatures (0-439-08747-3)
Text copyright © 2000 by Melvin Berger.

Snap! A Book About Alligators and Crocodiles (0-439-31746-0)
Text copyright © 2001 by Melvin & Gilda Berger.

All rights reserved. Published by Scholastic Inc.
SCHOLASTIC, CARTWHEEL BOOKS, and associated logos
are trademarks and/or registered trademarks of Scholastic Inc.

ISBN 0-439-84802-4

12 11 10 9 8 7 6 5 4 3 2 1   6 7 8 9 10 11/0
Printed in the U.S.A. 24 • This collection first printing, June 2006

CHOMP!
A Book About Sharks

by Melvin Berger

CHAPTER ONE

Great Hunters

Sharks are fish.

Most are very large.

They have huge appetites.

And they're almost always hunting for something to eat.

This hungry shark is swimming slowly back and forth.

Its senses are wide awake.

Suddenly the shark smells something.
It is blood in the water.
The blood is about a mile away.
That's as long as 20 blocks.
The shark speeds toward the smell.

The shark also picks up some faraway
sounds.
The shark's ears are two small holes
in the skin.
It hears something moving in the water.
The shark swims even faster.

The water is dark.

But the shark sees well in little light.

It spots an injured seal.

The seal has been badly cut.

There is blood in the water.

The shark circles around.

It comes in closer and closer.

Suddenly the shark lunges.

CHOMP!

It sinks its teeth into the seal.

The shark rips off a large chunk
of flesh.

GULP!

The shark swallows it whole.

All at once, other sharks appear.
They churn and shake the water.
Each wants the same seal.

The sharks snap and rip at the seal.
They bite each other.
Sometimes they even bite themselves!
It's called a "feeding frenzy."

Soon there is little left of the seal.
The feeding frenzy is over.
The sharks glide away.

Most sharks hunt fish, seals, and
porpoises.
But some eat dead or dying animals
and shellfish.
A few kinds of sharks feed on tiny sea
plants and animals.

CHAPTER TWO

Powerful Swimmers

Sharks seem made for swimming.
Most have sleek, rounded bodies.
They slip easily through the water.

Sharks use their fins to swim.
The big tail fin swings from side to side.
The tail pushes against the water.
It moves the shark forward.
The other fins keep the shark steady
in the water.

Sharks do not have smooth scales like most fish.

Instead they have many sharp, pointed scales.

The points face back toward the tail.

They help water flow over the shark's body—without slowing it down.

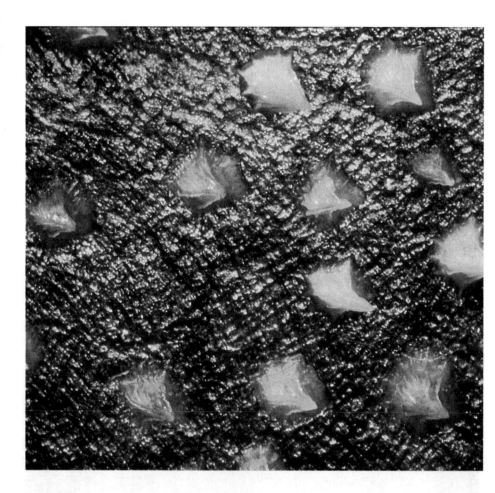

Sharks usually swim about three miles
per hour.
But they can put on bursts of speed.
When hunting, some reach 40 miles
per hour!

Did you know that most sharks swim
all the time?
They swim day and night.
They even swim when asleep!

Swimming and breathing go together.
If sharks stop swimming, they stop
breathing.
And they die.

Sharks breathe oxygen (say "OCK-suh-jun").
We breathe oxygen, too.
Our oxygen comes from the air.
Sharks get their oxygen from the water.

Most sharks swim with open mouths.
Water enters.
It flows over their gills.
The gills take the oxygen from the water.
Then the water flows out.

Swimming also keeps sharks afloat.
If they stop swimming, they sink to
the bottom.

A shark twists and turns as it swims.
That's because it doesn't have a bone
in its body!
A shark's skeleton is made of cartilage
(say "CAR-ti-luj").
And cartilage bends easily.

Your nose has cartilage.
See how easily you can twist and
turn it.

Sharks often swim with two types of
trusty friends.
One is the pilot fish.
Pilot fish seem to lead the sharks.
But all they do is catch food that the
sharks drop.

The other friend is the remora.
Remoras hitch rides on sharks.
They also eat shellfish that dig into the
sharks' skin.
No wonder sharks don't seem to mind
remoras tagging along.

CHAPTER THREE

Hundreds of Teeth

Sharks have lots of teeth.

Some have hundreds.

A few have thousands.

Imagine brushing that many teeth!

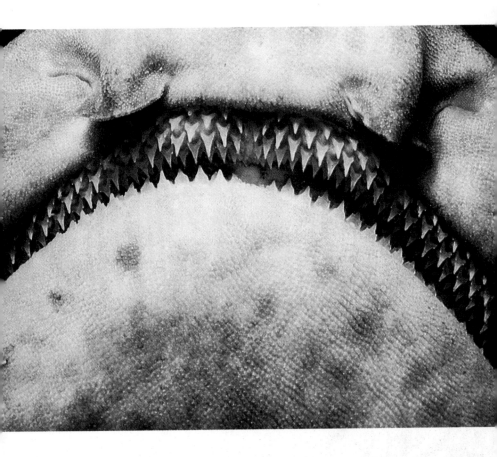

Shark teeth are not in one row like yours.
Sharks have as many as 20 rows
of teeth.
The rows are behind each other.

When a shark is ready to eat, it lifts
its snout.
This pushes the shark's mouth out
in front.
It also bares its teeth.

Sharks have teeth that are fit for what they eat.

- Curved teeth are for biting.
- Pointed teeth are for catching small fish.
- Flat teeth are for crushing shellfish.

Shark teeth do not have roots like yours.
Their teeth often break or fall out.
Then new teeth move up from the
row behind.
They take the place of the lost teeth.

Sharks can lose thousands of teeth in
a lifetime.
Divers find many on the ocean floor.
Sailors used to shave with them!

CHAPTER FOUR

Fantastic Babies

Shark babies are called pups.
Shark mothers usually give birth to a
few pups at a time.

All pups grow from eggs.
In most sharks, the eggs grow inside
the mother.
They can grow there for nearly a year.

When ready, the pups come out of the
mother's body.
But they're not like human babies.
Pups take care of themselves from
the start.
Off they go, to begin the hunt for food.

Some mother sharks lay eggs outside
their bodies.

The eggs are in cases.

The cases fall to the bottom of the sea.

The pup grows inside the egg case.

When it hatches, the pup swims out —
and away!

Sometimes egg cases wash ashore.

People find them on the beach.

They call the cases "mermaids' purses."

CHAPTER FIVE

Curious Creatures

Sharks live all over the world.

- They live in deep water and shallow water.
- They live in cold water and warm water.
- Some even live in rivers and lakes.

Nearly everyone is afraid of sharks.
Yet most rarely harm us.

The **great white shark** swims mainly
in deep, cold seas.
Its underside is white.
But its back is dark.
This makes the great white hard to see.
- From below, the shark looks like
  the sky.
- From above, the shark looks like
  the water.

Large animals, such as sea lions, fall
prey to the great white shark.

The **bull shark** is mostly found in shallow water.
Sometimes it swims into rivers or lakes.
A short snout and stout body make it look like a bull.
That's how it got its name.

The **blue shark** is easy to spot.
It lives in the deepest part of the ocean.
Yet it swims near the surface.
Its fins stick up out of the water.
Blues often swim together in large groups.

Some people call the **tiger shark**
a "swimming garbage can."
It will eat just about anything.
A fisherman once caught a tiger shark.
In its belly he found

- nine shoes,
- a belt,
- and a pair of pants!

One of the smallest sharks is the
dwarf shark.

It is only about six inches long.

You could hold one in your hand.

The biggest shark is the **whale shark**.
It can be as long and heavy as a
tractor trailer!
Sometimes the whale shark stands
upright in the water.
It bobs up and down, swallowing whole
schools of small fish.

The **hammerhead shark** looks odd,
to say the least.
It has a thick bar across the front of
its head.
And its eyes are at the ends of the bar.
No one is sure why.

It's easy to mistake the **carpet shark** for a rug.

It lays still on the ocean bottom.

Fringes around its snout make it look messy.

But let a fish swim by.

The carpet shark whips around and grabs it!

The **angel shark** is no angel.

It hides in reefs or caves under the water.

Or it digs its body into the sand.

Nearby shellfish have to be careful.

The angel shark is always ready to pounce.

Now you know.
Sharks

- are mighty hunters,
- are powerful swimmers,
- have lots of teeth,
- give birth to pups,
- live almost everywhere,
- and come in all sizes and shapes.

They're really amazing!

A Book About Whales and Dolphins

by Melvin & Gilda Berger

CHAPTER 1
As Big as Big Can Be

All whales are big.

But the blue whale is the BIGGEST.

- It's as high as a two-story building!
- It's as long as three buses!
- It's as heavy as twenty-five elephants!

The blue whale is the biggest animal
that ever lived.
It is even bigger than *Tyrannosaurus rex*!

Dolphins belong to the same family as whales.
But most dolphins are not as big as
most whales.

Whales look like fish.
But they're not fish.
Whales are mammals
- like dogs and cats,
- like cows and horses,
- and like you.

Like other mammals,
a baby whale is born alive.
It is born in shallow water,
tail first.

It may weigh
as much as 4,000
pounds at birth.
A baby whale is
called a calf.

At first the calf rolls
in the water like a barrel.
But the mother quickly turns it right side up.
Other whales help her push it to the surface.
And the calf takes its first breath of air.

The newborn calf feeds, or nurses,
from its mother's nipple.
The nipple squirts rich milk
into the baby's mouth.

The young calf nurses about 40 times a day.
Every day, it guzzles about 130 gallons
of milk.
And every day it gains about 200 pounds!
Soon the calf is ready to find its own food.

A whale is warm-blooded.
That means it stays warm, no matter
how cold the water.
Two heavy layers cover its body
like a blanket.
The top layer is the whale's skin.
It can be more than one foot thick!
Underneath is a layer of fat.
It is called blubber.
The blubber can be two feet thick!

You may know that a whale breathes air.
But it does not have a nose like yours.
Instead, a whale breathes through
an opening called a blowhole.
The blowhole is on top of the whale's head.
This lets the whale breathe while most
of its body stays underwater.

When a whale dives, it holds its breath.
One breath goes a long way.
Some whales can hold their breath
for up to two hours.
Try holding your breath.
One minute is tops!

Sooner or later, a whale must breathe.

Up it swims to the surface.

It breathes out the air in its lungs.

One day, you may see a whale
breathe out.

The air mixes with water.

It makes a cloud called a blow.

Not all blows are alike.

Some go straight up.

They can reach as high as a three-story building.

Others spread out in a spray.

They look like a fountain against the sky.

You can see some blows for miles.

You can hear them for hundreds of feet.

And if you're close, you can smell them.

Most whales have very bad breath!

Deep ocean water is dark and murky.
It is hard for whales to see very far.
But sound travels very well through water.
So whales depend more on hearing
than on sight.

Whales have ears,
but the ears are hard to spot.
They are two tiny holes in the skin.
Yet, whales hear better than most people.

Whales can hear the different sounds
that other whales make.
They can hear one another miles apart.
The sounds help them keep in touch.

Sounds help whales in another way.
They let whales find objects underwater.
The whale makes the sounds.
Then it listens for the echoes that bounce back.

Some echoes come back quickly.
That means the object is close.
Some echoes take longer to return.
That means the object is far away.
Using sound to find things is called
echolocation (ek-oh-loh-KAY-shun).

CHAPTER 2
Whales With Teeth

Most whales have teeth.

They are called **toothed whales**.

The teeth are for catching prey.

They are not for chewing.

Toothed whales swallow their food whole
and alive.

The **sperm whale** is the biggest toothed whale.

It's a huge animal in many ways. It has

- the biggest head of any whale,
- the largest brain,
- the thickest skin,
- and the heaviest layer of blubber.

Fifty giant teeth line the sperm whale's lower jaw.

Each is several inches long.

And each weighs half a pound.

The sperm whale eats many kinds of fish.

But its favorite food looks like an octopus.

It is called a **squid**.

Instead of eight arms, a squid has ten arms.

Squid come in all sizes.

Some are as small as cucumbers.

Others are as big as canoes.

The biggest ones are called **giant squid**.

Sperm whales hunt giant squid.

The squid live at the bottom of the sea.

Sperm whales dive very deep
to catch them.

Down a sperm whale drops
like a sleek submarine.

After about a mile, it nears the ocean floor.

It uses echolocation to find its prey.

A sperm whale can't always catch
a giant squid.

But when it does, the squid fights back.

The whale and squid battle it out.

But the whale usually wins.

It swallows the huge creature.

Narwhals are much smaller than sperm whales.

Most have only two teeth.

In male narwhals, one tooth sticks straight out.

It is eight feet long and comes to a sharp point.

The tooth is called a tusk.

No one knows why narwhals have tusks. Are they used

- to spear large fish?
- to dig shellfish out of the mud on the ocean bottom?
- to attract females?

The answer is a mystery.

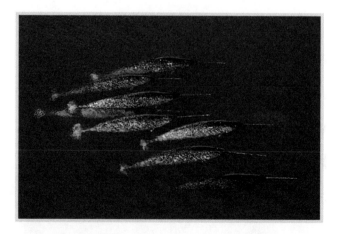

CHAPTER 3
Dolphins

Dolphins are small, toothed whales.
They are the biggest group of whales
with teeth.

Sailors tell about dolphins saving people.
Some years ago, a woman fell out
of her boat.
Three dolphins swam over.
They held her up in the water.
And they pushed her onto a beach.

Dolphins help each other in the same way.
Let's say one dolphin in a group is sick
or hurt.
The others carry it through the water.
They lift it to the surface to breathe.
They protect it against enemies.

Dolphins are playful.
They leap and turn in the water.
The young rub up against each other.
They play underwater tag.

People like to hear dolphins "talk."
Each bark, squeal, squawk, or whistle
seems to mean something different.
Scientists listen carefully to these sounds.
They try to discover the meanings.

You may know **bottle-nose dolphins** best.
Often you see them in water parks
and aquariums.
Their beaks make them look smiling
and happy.

Bottle-noses seem to be very smart.
Trainers can teach them to play basketball
or to jump through hoops.
One bottle-nose was the star of a TV show.

The **common dolphin** is smaller than
the bottle-nose.
It's also a better swimmer.

Common dolphins often swim
alongside ships.
They keep up with them, mile after mile.
From time to time, the dolphins leap
and flip in midair!

The biggest dolphin is the **orca**.
It mainly feeds on fish and squid.
But the orca also attacks other whales.
And it makes meals of penguins, seals,
and walruses.
No wonder some people call the orca
"killer whale."

Orcas hunt blue whales for their great
big tongues!

The tongue of a blue whale is an orca's favorite food.

Orcas live in all the world's oceans.
Someday you may spot one
from far away.
You'll see a six-foot-high fin sticking up
from its back.
It's a sight you'll never forget!

CHAPTER 4
Toothless Wonders

The largest whales have no teeth.
Instead, hundreds of fuzzy plates hang down
from their upper jaws.
The plates are called **baleen** (buh-LEEN).
They look and feel like giant fingernails.
And they act like oversize strainers.

The **blue whale** is the largest baleen whale.
As it swims, it opens its gigantic mouth
very wide.
Tons of water flow right in.

The water holds millions of small,
shrimplike creatures, or **krill**.

The whale closes its mouth.
Down come the baleen.
With its tongue, the whale squeezes
the water out through the baleen.
But the krill get stuck.
And the whale swallows its dinner.

The blue whale has an amazing appetite.
In one day, it gulps down about four tons
of krill!

The **humpback whale** is another baleen whale.

You may think the humpback whale has a hump on its back.

It does not.

The whale just humps, or shows its neck and back, when it dives!

Every now and then the humpback flip-flops in the air.

It is called breaching.

The whale suddenly leaps out of the water.

Its long, white flippers spread out like wings.

Then the humpback falls back into the water.

SPLASH!

The landing sounds like an exploding firecracker.

Humpback whales are the opera singers
of the ocean.

Their "songs" last up to 20 minutes.

Each group of whales repeats its own song
over and over again.

They never seem to get tired.

Right whales got their name long ago. Whalers said they were the "right" ones to hunt.

They were slow swimmers and easy to catch.

And their bodies held lots of the oil that the whalers wanted.

Long ago, many right whales swam in the oceans.

But hunters killed them in great numbers.

Sad to say, few are left.

You can also tell a right whale
from far away.
Its blow is divided.
It looks like the letter V.

Sometimes right whales are
like sailboats.
Instead of sails, the whales raise
their tails in the air.
Their "sail-tails" catch the wind.
The wind pushes the whales from deep
to shallow water — and back again.

Right whales sometimes beat the water with their tails.

Or, they jump from the water and crash back with a mighty splash.

Sometimes one starts.

Then others follow.

Scientists wonder:

- Are the whales being playful?
- Are they keeping in touch with each other?
- Or are they looking for something good to eat?

CHAPTER 5
From Sea to Shining Sea

Whales live in all the oceans of the world.
Most swim in groups called pods.
Pods have from three to hundreds
of whales.

Some whales spend part of the year
in warm waters.
In summer, they migrate, or move.
They migrate to the cold waters
near the North and South poles.

Day and night, the pod swims slowly
through the water.
The trip may take several months.
The whales hardly stop to sleep or eat.
In case of trouble, they help each other.

The whales stay in the cold waters
for about three months.
The waters have lots of food.
Every day, the whales take in huge
amounts of krill and other sea creatures.
Their blubber gets very thick.

In time, the water begins to freeze.
The whales migrate back to warm water
before they get trapped by the ice.

Finally, they reach the warm waters.
Here the pregnant females give birth.
The mother whale stays close to her calf.
And she looks out for danger.

While in the warm waters, the whales
stop eating.
They live off the fat of their blubber.

Soon it is summer again.
The whales gather in groups.
They start their long journey back
to the cold waters.

From time to time, a whale swims
onto a beach.
The whale is said to be stranded.

The stranded whale must find its way back
into the sea.
Out of the water, whales find it hard
to breathe.

Sometimes other whales hear the cries
of a stranded whale.
They come to its aid.
Then they become stranded, too.

Stranded whales often live for several days.
They may even get back into the water.
Many times, people help.
If not, the stranded whales die.

Not long ago, a young whale was stranded.
The U.S. Coast Guard found it.

They named it Humphrey.

The sailors towed Humphrey
into shallow water.

Doctors examined the whale.

They found many germs in its blowhole.

So they gave the whale medicine.

In ten days, Humphrey was ready
to swim out to sea.
Boats and swimmers helped the whale
swim safely away.

One day you may find a stranded whale.
Call for help.
While waiting, keep away from the whale.
Then maybe your whale will live happily
ever after — just like Humphrey!

DIVE!

A BOOK OF DEEP-SEA CREATURES

by Melvin Berger

CHAPTER ONE

Down to the Bottom

Would you like to visit the bottom
of the sea?
It's easy.
Just climb aboard a little submarine.
Take your seat—and let's go!

The submarine dives down below
the surface.
At first the water is bright blue.
It sparkles in the sunlight.
There are many fish.

As the submarine drops deeper
and deeper, the water gets very dark.
The sun's rays don't reach this far.
Fewer fish swim here.

Finally, the submarine is one mile
under the sea.
The water is darker than
the darkest night.

BUMP!
The submarine lands on the ocean bottom
and shines a bright light.
The sea floor is muddy.
It's covered with fish bones and
broken shells.
The water, if you could feel it,
is freezing cold.

Very few plants and animals live here.
How odd they look!
Like beings from another planet.
Welcome to the weird and wonderful
world of deep-sea creatures!

CHAPTER TWO

Flashing Lights

The sea is black.

But look closely and you'll see tiny lights

darting this way and that.

The lights come from animals that

live here.

Most of these animals make their own

light from chemicals inside their bodies.

The light acts like bait.

It attracts prey, or other creatures,

which the animals like to eat.

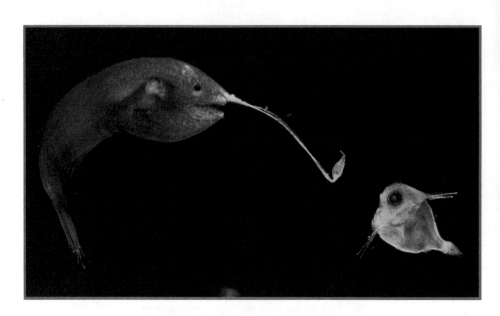

The **angler fish** lives near the bottom of the ocean.
The female has a long rod that hangs from her head.
It looks like a fishing pole.
But instead of a worm at the end, the pole has a light.

Other fish swim toward the light.
When one gets close, the angler fish snatches it in her mouth.
Good-bye fish!

The angler fish has something else
on her head.

It's the much, much smaller male
angler fish!

He attaches himself to her.

And he stays there for the rest of his life.

A very close couple!

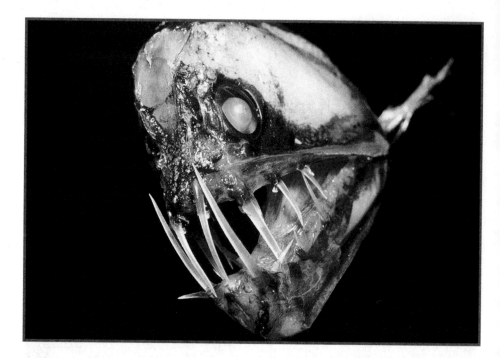

Viper fish dangle an outside light
like angler fish.
But some viper fish have extra lights.
These lights are *inside* the mouth!

The viper fish swims with its mouth
open wide.
The lights attract small fish.
They head for the bright spots.
Before you know it, the hungry viper fish
gulps down the fish.

The **hatchet fish** has no light on a pole.
Instead, rows of light line the bottom
of its body.
The lights sparkle as the hatchet fish
swims.

Some fish rush over to get a better look.
That's a mistake.
The hatchet fish twists around with jaws
wide open.
In one bite, the fish swallows its prey.

Flashlight fish also give off light.
But they don't make the light themselves.
The light comes from glowing germs,
or bacteria, inside their body.

Flashlight fish have two see-through bags
under their eyes.
That's where the glowing bacteria live.
The fish cannot switch off the bacteria.
But they can cover them with a layer
of skin.

The light helps protect the flashlight fish.

Suppose it sees an enemy.

The flashlight fish swims in a straight line
with lights on.

Then it covers them up.

Quickly the flashlight fish turns.

Surprise!

The enemy can't find it.

The fish swims safely away.

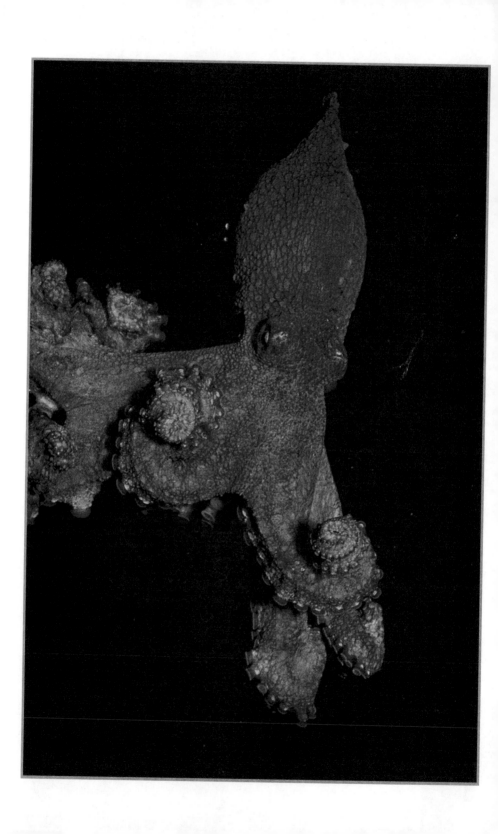

CHAPTER THREE

Huge Eyes and Wagging Arms

Many deep-sea creatures have
huge eyes.

Can you guess why?

The bigger their eyes, the better they
can see in the dark.

Certain octopuses live in very
deep water.

They have two great, big eyes that
help them spot their prey.

Eight arms stretch out from the head of an octopus.

Each arm has two rows of small, round suckers.

They can grab and hold anything.

If an octopus loses an arm, a new one grows in its place.

Squid are like octopuses.

Each has two gigantic eyes.

Around a squid's head are ten arms —
eight long ones plus two extra-long ones.

The arms have suckers to catch prey.

A squid swims in an odd way.
It fills parts of its body with water and
then forces the water out.
This shoots the squid forward, much like
a jet plane.

When the squid spots a fish's lights,
it whips out its arms.
The arms trap the fish.
The squid pops the fish into its mouth.

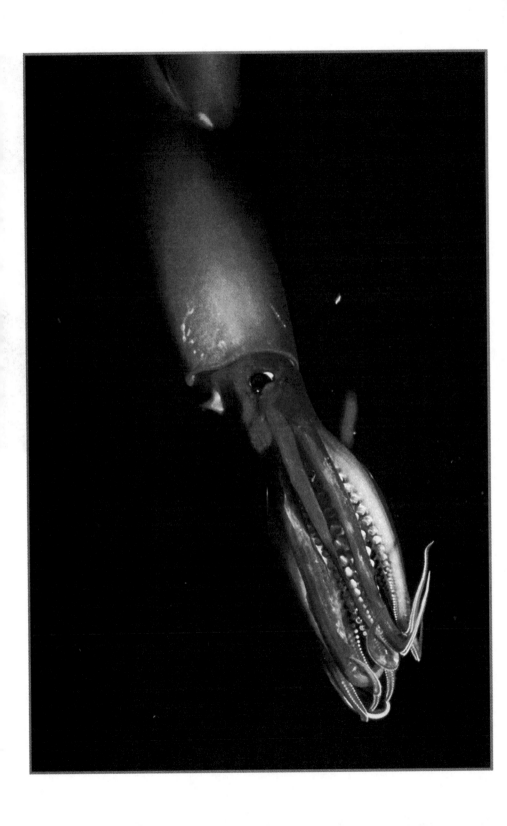

The **giant squid** is the largest squid
of all.
Its body can grow longer than
a big bus!

This dark red deep-sea creature has
the largest eyes of any animal on earth.
Each is the size of a car's hubcap!

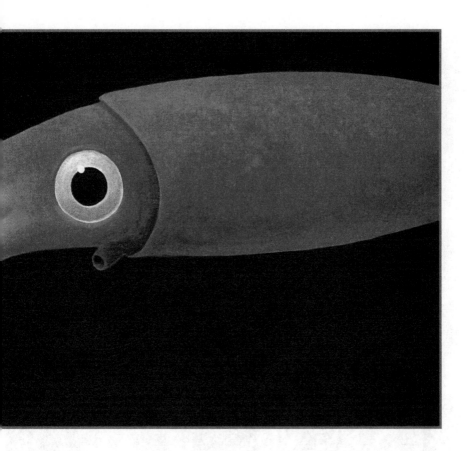

The squid's tongue is not for licking.
Its tongue has teeth!
The squid uses it for chewing.

Sailors used to tell of huge monsters
that lived in the sea.
Now we think those monsters were
really giant squid!

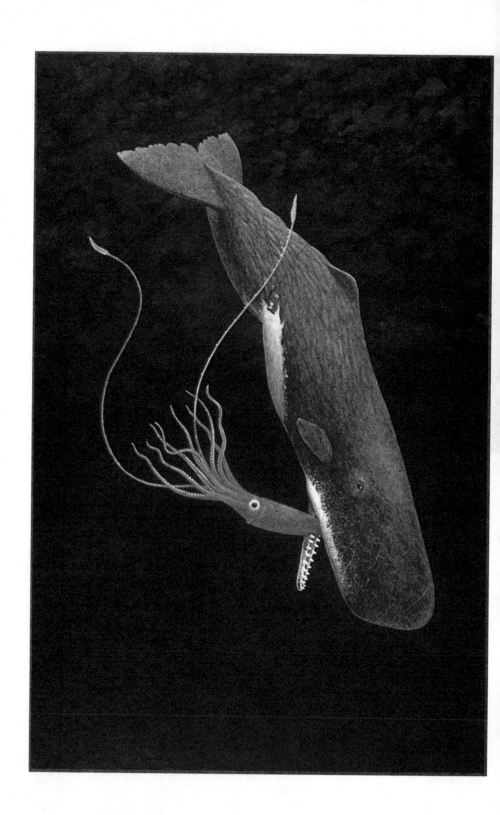

CHAPTER FOUR

Deep-sea Diver

The giant squid fears only one deep-sea
animal — the mighty **sperm whale**.
This whale eats many different
sea creatures.
But its favorite is the giant squid.

The sperm whale is like other whales.
It goes up to the surface to breathe air.
Yet it also feeds on squid
at the ocean bottom.
How does the sperm whale do this?
It's a deep-sea diver!

The sperm whale first fills its huge lungs
with air.
Then it holds its breath and plunges down,
head first.
After a mile or so, the whale comes to rest
on the ocean floor.
It stops and waits.

If the whale is lucky, a giant squid swims by.
The whale slams its mouth shut
on one of the squid's arms.
The squid puts up a fight.

The whale and the squid are about the
same length.
But the whale is much heavier.
It swallows the squid in one gulp —
whole and alive!
But the squid keeps on fighting.
It cuts and scratches the whale's stomach
leaving scars inside.

A sperm whale can only stay in deep
water for about an hour.
Then it needs to breathe.
The whale swims to the surface
and breathes out.
Its warm breath forms a mist
that sprays up like a fountain.

After a while, the whale takes another
deep breath.
And down it plunges.

CHAPTER FIVE

Big Mouths and
Elastic Stomachs

Life is hard in deep water.

It can be a long time between meals.

Once in a great while, there's lots to eat.

Then the fish want to gobble up

all they can.

Large mouths and elastic stomachs are

a big help.

Fish near the ocean bottom are

usually small.

But many have mouths that can open

real wide.

Their jaws swing far apart.

They can swallow prey twice their size!

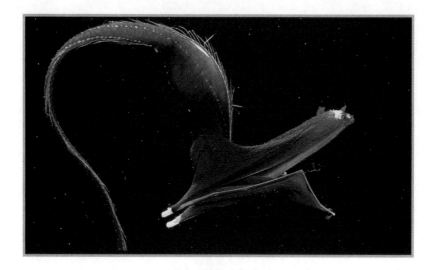

The mouth of the **gulper eel** is the biggest part of its body.
The rest is long and thin like a tail.
A small, red light at the end looks like a taillight on a car.

The taillight attracts prey.
The jaws take care of the rest.
Dozens of small, sharp teeth hold the victim.
Then the gulper swallows it whole.

As the gulper eats, its belly grows larger and larger.
It can double in size!

The **great swallower** also has a huge mouth and an elastic stomach.
You can guess how it got its name.
It's only about six inches long.
Yet this fish can swallow prey almost twice its size.

Sometimes the great swallower stuffs itself with food.
The skin over its belly stretches very thin.
Look closely and you can see its last meal inside!

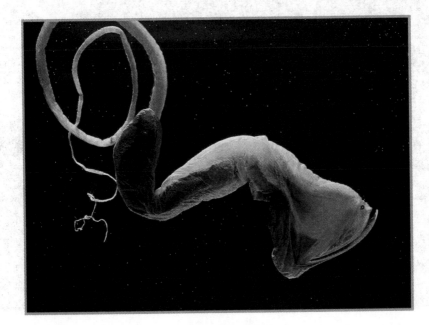

CHAPTER SIX

The Ocean Floor

The ocean floor has few signs of life.

But the creatures that do live here are

very strange.

Most bizarre is the **tripod fish**.

It walks!

The tripod walks on three "legs" —

its two stiff side fins and tail.

They lift the fish off the ocean floor.

Best of all, they let it catch shrimp that

swim just above the ocean bottom.

The **ratfish** looks a little like a shark.
It digs in the mud for creatures that
hide there.
Sometimes it finds bits of food buried
in the ooze.

Male ratfish attract females
in an odd way.
They make loud drumming sounds.
If a female likes the beat, she swims over.

Sea cucumbers look like garden cucumbers with legs.

But they're animals, not vegetables.

These tubby creatures live in large groups.

In the mud, they find what they like to eat.

Fish and crabs prey on sea cucumbers.

But these enemies had better watch out.

When in danger, sea cucumbers squirt out long, sticky tubes.

The tubes tangle up the enemy.

And they give the sea cucumber a chance to escape.

Sea pens are like sea cucumbers.
Large numbers live together on the
ocean floor.
Each sea pen looks like an old-fashioned
quill or feather pen.
Rooted to one spot, they wait to have
their food delivered.
Each snatches small bits of food
from the water around it.

Also stuck in the sea floor are
sea squirts.
Their name comes from the way they
take in water, pull out any tiny creatures,
and squirt out the rest of the water.

CHAPTER SEVEN

Black Smokers

Deep water is icy cold — except in a very few places.

Here, cold water seeps down through cracks in the ocean floor.

The heat inside the earth warms the water.

The warm water bubbles up through "chimneys," called black smokers.

Tubeworms cluster around these
warm spots.
The creatures live inside tall, thin,
white tubes stuck to the ocean floor.
They make the tubes from sand
and material from their own bodies.

The tubes protect them from crabs
and other enemies.
The tallest are about the height
of a tall man.
Tubeworms don't have to look for food.
Bacteria in their body make food
for them.
The bacteria get chemicals
from the water around the smokers.
The chemicals feed the bacteria,
which become food for the tubeworms.

Deep-sea shrimp also count on bacteria
for food.
These bacteria live in their mouth.
They take in chemicals that the shrimp
scrapes loose from the ocean floor.
The chemicals feed the bacteria,
which become food for the shrimp.

Even a submarine can't stay underwater forever.

It's time to leave the deep-sea creatures with —

- flashing lights,
- huge eyes and wagging arms,
- big mouths and elastic stomachs,
- three "legs," and
- bodies stuck in the mud.

Let's hope we see them again soon!

SNAP!

A Book About Alligators and Crocodiles

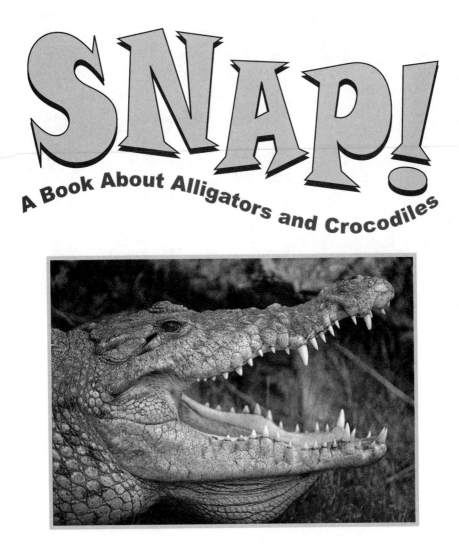

by Melvin & Gilda Berger

CHAPTER 1
Lumpy and Bumpy

A giant alligator floats in the water.
You can hardly see its body.
Most of it is hidden.
You might think it's a lumpy, bumpy log.

Look carefully.
Can you spot the alligator's eyes?
They stick up above the water.
They let the alligator see all around.

The alligator's nostrils also stick up
above the water.
That's a very good thing.
The alligator can breathe and hide
under the water at the same time!

The alligator lies still.
It waits and watches.
In a while, a very large fish swims by.

Suddenly the alligator flings open its
huge jaws.
SNAP!
It catches the fish with its many sharp teeth.
The fish tries to break free.
But the alligator holds on tightly.

Soon the fish stops wriggling.
The alligator juggles the fish around
in its jaws.
It gets the fish into the right place
for swallowing.
The alligator jerks back its head.
And the fish slides down its throat!

The alligator swims to the riverbank.

It slowly climbs out of the water.

It walks on its four short legs.

Its long tail drags behind.

Suppose you happened to walk by.

You might think the alligator is a crocodile.

The animals look much alike.

How can you tell an alligator from
a crocodile?

CHAPTER 2
Alike, but Different

The alligator has a long, lumpy,
bumpy body.
So does the crocodile.
The alligator has four short legs, sharp
teeth, and a long, strong tail.
So does the crocodile.

But alligators and crocodiles are not
exact look-alikes.
They have different noses, or snouts.

An alligator has a wide, rounded snout.
It looks like the letter U.
A crocodile's snout comes to a point.
It looks more like the letter V.

There is another important difference.
It is the fourth tooth on the bottom jaw.
In both animals, this tooth is extra long.
But the tooth fits inside the alligator's
upper jaw.
And it sticks up outside the crocodile's
jaw.

Crocodiles are usually longer than alligators.
They can also outswim alligators.
Most crocodiles weigh more, too.
That may be why crocodiles are better fighters.

Alligators and crocodiles often wait quietly for their dinner.
They lie hidden in the water.
They wait for animals they want to eat.

Both alligators and crocodiles live in lakes, swamps, and rivers.
But alligators live only in the southern United States or in China.
You can find crocodiles all over the world.

CHAPTER 3
Mothers and Babies

It's spring.

The alligators and crocodiles are starting to build their nests.

The nests are on land.

But they are always near water.

The female alligator shovels with her hind legs.

She scoops grass, twigs, and leaves into a big heap.

Soon she has a huge nest.

It may be as big as a king-sized bed.

And it may be as tall as a first grader.

The alligator then crawls all over the nest.

She packs it down with her heavy body.

The crocodile usually makes a more
simple nest.

She just digs a hole in the sand.

Or, she makes a pile of twigs, grass,
and mud.

The female alligator or crocodile lays from 20 to 60 eggs in her nest.
The eggs are white.
They look like the eggs you buy in a store.
But they are bigger.

The female does not sit on the eggs.
The sun warms the nest.
And the female keeps guard.
She watches out for bears, skunks, and lizards.
These are some of the animals that eat alligator and crocodile eggs.

Sometimes an animal tries to steal
some eggs.
The mother attacks.
Most enemies will run away.
The mother's sharp teeth and powerful
jaws are very scary!

Two or three months pass.
The mother hears chirps from inside
the eggshells!
That tells her the eggs are ready
to hatch.
She digs the eggs out from the nest.
And she helps the babies break out
of their shells.

Sometimes the babies crawl into the mother's mouth.
She gently carries them to the water.
Then she opens her mouth.
Out they crawl.

A female alligator or crocodile seems to be a good mom.
She stays close to her babies for a year or more.
The mother protects her babies.
If an enemy comes close, she hisses or roars.

The mother gives her babies piggyback
rides.
She lets them sit on her head.
But she does not feed them.
The babies must find their own food.

Luckily for them, babies have full sets of teeth.

The teeth are like tiny needles.

The babies use them to catch small fish, tadpoles, flies, moths, and beetles.

The baby alligators and crocodiles grow
very quickly.
Some gain about a foot a year
for six years.
Suppose you grew that fast.
You'd be around seven feet tall!

CHAPTER 4
Day and Night

Alligators and crocodiles nap on and off
all day.
Sometimes they sleep in the water.
Other times they rest on riverbanks.

The alligators and crocodiles lie
in the sun.
Their thick skin collects the rays.
The sun warms their bodies.
Alligators and crocodiles are cold-blooded
animals.

Cold-blooded animals must get heat
from outside their bodies.
Without outside heat, the animals move
very slowly.

So, alligators and crocodiles live in warm
parts of the world.
And they bask in the sun.
When they get too hot, the animals head
for the shade.
Sometimes they go back into the water.

Alligators and crocodiles must look
for animals to eat.
These animals are called prey.
Fish, birds, turtles, frogs, and raccoons
are favorite prey.
So are large animals, such as pigs,
deer, dogs, sheep, and cows.

Suppose a crocodile spots a wildebeest
(WILL-deh-beest) crossing a river.
The crocodile clamps its jaws down
on its prey.
SNAP!
The wildebeest cannot escape.

Sometimes the crocodile grips the
wildebeest in its jaws.
It drags the wildebeest under the water.
The wildebeest drowns.
Then, the crocodile tears it apart.
The crocodile swallows the pieces
whole — without chewing!

Alligators and crocodiles usually eat
their prey in the water.
Special flaps of skin keep the water out
as they eat.
Other flaps cover their ears and
nostrils.

Alligators and crocodiles also have extra eyelids.

They're like goggles.

They protect the animals' eyes underwater.

Yet, the animal can still see.

The teeth of alligators and crocodiles are special.

The front ones are very sharp.

The animals use them for catching and holding their prey.

The teeth in the back are short and blunt.

Alligators and crocodiles use them to get the food in place before swallowing.

Alligators and crocodiles lose many teeth.
Some get knocked out by their prey.
Others become worn and fall out.

Alligators may lose 3,000 teeth in a
lifetime!
But new teeth are growing in all the time.
One tooth falls out.
And a new one pops up to take its place!

Alligators and crocodiles look slow and lazy.

But they swim very fast.

When chasing prey, an alligator or crocodile can top 20 miles an hour.

That's almost five times the speed of the fastest human swimmer!

On land they run only half as fast.

Believe it or not—
alligators and crocodiles have
good manners!
Let's say a crocodile catches a cow.
It tears off a chunk of flesh.
And it swims away to enjoy its meal.

Other crocodiles swim over.
They rip into the cow.
In a while, the first crocodile returns.
But it waits its turn to eat again!

Alligators and crocodiles do not eat
every day.
Once a week is more usual.
Some can go without food for as long
as two years!
How can they go so long without
eating?
They store lots of fat in their bodies.
Most of the fat ends up in their tails.

Chemicals in their stomachs break down the food alligators and crocodiles eat. This helps the animals digest what they swallow.
Remember: Alligators and crocodiles do not chew their food!

Alligators and crocodiles also swallow pebbles.
It's not because pebbles taste good.
The pebbles weigh them down.
They help the animals float just under the surface of the water and keep them out of sight.

Some birds are safe around crocodiles.

Among them are white herons and plovers.

They often ride on top of alligators and crocodiles.

The birds pick at tiny bugs they find there.

A plover may even hop into a crocodile's mouth!

It acts like a toothpick.

The plover pecks out bits of food from between the crocodile's teeth!

The plover gets something to eat.

And the crocodile gets a clean mouth.

CHAPTER 5
All in the Family

Alligators and crocodiles are cousins.
They belong to a family of animals called
crocodilians (krok-uh-DILL-yuns).
The crocodilian family also includes
gharials (GARE-ee-uhlz) and **caiman**
(KAY-mun).

Gharials are sometimes called **gavials** (GAY-vee-uhlz).

They look most like crocodiles.

Gharials live only in Asia.

Caiman look more like alligators.
They live in warm parts of North and
South America.

Crocodilians are a very old family.
They lived at the time of the dinosaurs.
That was over 200 million years ago!

Today, there are two kinds of alligators —
the American alligator and the Chinese
alligator.
They live thousands of miles apart.
But they look very much alike.

The American alligator has a huge tail.
It is sometimes a powerful weapon.
One blow can kill a large enemy.
It can even kill a human being.

The Chinese alligator is smaller than the American alligator.

This animal is rare.

There are only about 500 left in the wild.

There are 12 different kinds of crocodiles. The American crocodile lives mostly in Florida and Central America.

It is far less common than the American alligator.

The saltwater crocodile of Asia and Australia is the biggest of all crocodilians.
One used to live in Australia's National Zoo. It weighed more than one ton!

The Nile crocodile lives in Africa.
Some Africans call it "the animal that kills while smiling."
Nile crocodiles actually harm more people than lions do!

Crocodilians are amazing creatures.
Their ancestors walked with the
dinosaurs.
Dinosaurs died out millions of years ago.
Yet crocodilians are still here.
Let's hope they're here to stay!

Dedications and Acknowledgments

Chomp! A Book About Sharks

For the boys and girls of the E. M. Baker School
— M.B.

Special thanks to Laurie Roulston of the Denver Museum
of Natural History for her expertise

Splash! A Book About Whales and Dolphins

For Max,
A great fan of Hello Reader! books
— M.B. and G.B.

Special thanks to Laurie Roulston of the Denver Museum
of Natural History for her expertise

Dive! A Book of Deep-Sea Creatures

For Jack and Selma, with love
— M.B.

Special thanks to Laurie Roulston of the Denver Museum
of Natural History for her expertise

Snap! A Book About Alligators and Crocodiles

For Hana, with much love
— M.B. and G.B.

Special thanks to Paul L. Sieswerda of The New York Aquarium
for his expertise

Photography and Illustration Credits

Chomp! A Book About Sharks

Cover and page 5: James D. Watt/Innerspace Visions; pages 3 and 39: Bob Cranston/Innerspace Visions; page 6: Ben Cropp/Innerspace Visions; page 7: Norbert Wu; page 8: Chris A. Crumley/EarthWater Stock Photography; page 9: Bill Curtsinger; pages 10-11: Mark Conlin/Innerspace Visions; page 12: Ron & Valerie Taylor/Innerspace Visions; page 13: Walt Stearns/Innerspace Visions; page 14: Norbert Wu/Peter Arnold, Inc.; page 15: Bill Curtsinger; page 16: Doug Perrine and Jose Castro/Innerspace Visions; page 17: Bill Curtsinger; page 19: Michael S. Nolan/Innerspace Visions; page 20: Michel Jozon/Innerspace Visions; page 21: Doug Perrine/Innerspace Visions; page 22: Mark Strickland/Innerspace Visions; pages 23-25: Jeff Rotman; page 26: Fred McConnaughey/Photo Researchers; page 27: Mark Strickland/Innerspace Visions; page 28: Doug Perrine/Innerspace Visions; page 29: Mark Conlin/Innerspace Visions; page 30: Massimo & Lucia Simion/Jeff Rotman; page 31: Jeff Rotman; page 32: Jeff Rotman/Innerspace Visions; page 33: David B. Fleetham/Innerspace Visions; page 34: Doug Perrine/Innerspace Visions; page 35: Bill Curtsinger; page 36: J. Dan Wright/EarthWater Stock Photography; page 37 top and bottom: Norbert Wu; page 38: Douglas Seifert/EarthWater Stock Photography; page 40: Nigel Marsh/Innerspace Visions; page 41: Mark Conlin/Innerspace Visions; page 42: Kelvin Aitken/Peter Arnold, Inc.

Splash! A Book About Whales and Dolphins

Page 43: Stone; pages 44-45: Mark Carwardine/Still Pictures/Peter Arnold, Inc.; pages 46-47: BIOS/Y. Lefevre/Peter Arnold, Inc.; page 48: Auscape/J-M LaRoque/Peter Arnold, Inc.; page 49: Kelvin Aitken/Peter Arnold, Inc.; page 50: George D. Lepp/Photo Researchers, Inc.; page 51: John Hyde/Bruce Coleman Inc.; page 52: François Gohier/Photo Researchers, Inc.; page 53: Art Wolfe/Photo Researchers, Inc.; pages 54-55: D. Perrine/Peter Arnold, Inc.; page 56: Michel Jozon/Innerspace Visions; page 57: Michael S. Nolan/Innerspace Visions; page 58 (top): Doug Perrine/Innerspace Visions; page 58 (bottom): Norbert Wu; page 60: Fred Bruemmer/Peter Arnold, Inc.; page 61: Windland Rice/Bruce Coleman Inc.; page 62: Doug Perrine/Peter Arnold, Inc.; page 63: Horst Schafer/Peter Arnold, Inc.; page 64: DiMaggio/Kalish/Peter Arnold, Inc.; page 65: Mike Couffer/Bruce Coleman, Inc.; pages 66-67: François Gohier/Photo Researchers, Inc.; page 68: Doc White/Innerspace Visions; page 69: Ingrid Visser/Innerspace Visions; page 71: Stuart Westmorland/Stone; pages 72-73: François Gohier/Photo Researchers, Inc.; page 74: Tom Brakefield/Bruce Coleman Inc.; page 75: Oswaldo Vasquez/Innerspace Visions; page 77: Marilyn Kazmers/Innerspace Visions; page 79: AP/Wide World Photos, Inc.; page 80: Ingrid Visser/Innerspace Visions.

Dive! A Book of Deep-Sea Creatures

Pages 81 and 90: Gregory Ochocki/Innerspace Visions, courtesy of Scripps Institution of Oceanography; page 82: Dale Stokes/Mo Yung Productions; page 85: Norbert Wu; page 86: Gregory Ochocki/Innerspace Visions, courtesy of Scripps Institution of Oceanography; pages 88-89, 91-94: Norbert Wu; page 96: Doug Perrine/Innerspace Visions; page 97: Bob Cranston/Innerspace Visions; page 98: James D. Watt/Innerspace Visions; page 99: Bob Cranston/Innerspace Visions; pages 100-102: Richard Ellis/Innerspace Visions; page 105: Michael S. Nolan/Innerspace Visions; page 106: Doug Perrine/Innerspace Visions; pages 108-110: Norbert Wu; page 112: David Fleetham/Innerspace Visions; page 113: Doug Perrine/Innerspace Visions; page 114: Andrew J. Martinez/Photo Researchers; page 115: B. Murton/Southampton Oceanography Centre/Science Photo Library/Photo Researchers; page 116: 1993 NSF Oasis Project/Norbert Wu; page 118: Norbert Wu.

Snap! A Book About Alligators and Crocodiles

Page 119: Tom McHugh/Photo Researchers, Inc.; pages 120-121: E. R. Degginger/Photo Researchers, Inc.; page 122: Jack Couffer/Bruce Coleman Inc.; page 123: Stephen J. Krasemann/Photo Researchers, Inc.; page 124: Alan D. Carey/Photo Researchers, Inc.; page 125: Tom & Pat Leeson/Photo Researchers, Inc.; page 127: David Austen/Stone; page 128: Robert Hermes/Photo Researchers, Inc.; page 129: Wendell Metzen/Bruce Coleman Inc.; page 130: Treat Davidson/Photo Researchers, Inc.; page 131: CC Lockwood/Photo Researchers, Inc.; page 132: Dr. Robert Potts Jr./Photo Researchers, Inc.; page 133: Wolfgang Bayer/Bruce Coleman Inc.; page 134: Nigel J. Dennis/Photo Researchers, Inc.; page 135 top: Roy Morsch/Bruce Coleman Inc.; page 135 bottom: Harold Hoffman/Photo Researchers, Inc.; page 136 top: Dr. Robert Potts Jr./Photo Researchers, Inc.; page 136 bottom: David T. Roberts/Nature's Images, Inc./Photo Researchers, Inc.; page 137: Bill Goulet/Bruce Coleman Inc.; pages 138-139: John Serrao/Photo Researchers, Inc.; page 140: James Prince/Photo Researchers, Inc.; page 141: Gary Retherford/Photo Researchers, Inc.; page 143: Charles V. Angelo/Photo Researchers, Inc.; page 144: Byron Jorjorian/Bruce Coleman Inc.; page 145: Stephen Cooper/Stone; page 146: Root/Okapia/PR/Photo Researchers, Inc.; page 148: Laura Riley/Bruce Coleman Inc.; page 149: The Purcell Team/CORBIS; pages 150-151: Larry Allan/Bruce Coleman Inc.; page 152: Frank Krahmer/Bruce Coleman Inc.; page 153: Gary Retherford/Photo Researchers, Inc.; page 154: Jeff Foott/Bruce Coleman Inc.; page 155 top: Bill Bachman/Photo Researchers, Inc.; page 155 bottom: Mary Beth Angelo/Photo Researchers, Inc.; page 156: Fritz Polking/Bruce Coleman Inc.; page 157: Mark Strickland/Innerspace Visions.

Back cover

Top: Byron Jorjorian/Bruce Coleman Inc.; *Chomp!* cover: James D. Watt/Innerspace Visions; *Splash!* cover: Kim Heacox/Peter Arnold, Inc.; *Dive!* cover: Norbert Wu; *Snap!* cover: Tom McHugh/Photo Researchers, Inc.